THE AFRICAN SYMBOLS

Symbolic Verses from Africa

Unveiling the Untold Stories of Africa

TABLE OF CONTENTS

Dedication 5

RETURN TO AFRICA 6

LEGACY OF SURVIVAL 8

REKINDLED BY NATURE 10

HARMONIES OF THE BAOBAB 11

SWEETNESS PERSONIFIED 13

THE RISE OF AFURIKA 14

THE BEAUTY OF MY BLACK SKIN 16

THE MIDNIGHT LAMENT 18

SERENADE OF KENYA 19

THE UNHEARD MAN 21

THE GUARDIANS EMBRACE 22

SYMPHONY OF ECHOING DRUMS 23

WHISPERS OF THE BAOBAB TREE 24

BECAUSE OF AFRICA 25

JUST LIKE THAT 29

IN THE REALM OF DREAMS 32

THE SMILE REBORN 33

THE AFRICAN HARVEST   35

EPIC OF BEAUTY   37

DON'T BREAK THE JAR OF OIL   39

ELYSIAN AND ABASSINIA   40

GO FOR MORE   42

EASY NANA   44

THE TANZANIAN WOMAN   46

NKECHI   48

ONE STEP AFTER THE OTHER   50

LEARN TO BE BETTER   52

THE RESEMBLANCE   53

CLIMB A GOOD TREE   55

AFRICAN PARTY   56

AFRICAN RHYTHMS   58

THE VILLAGE'S EMBRACE   60

EMANCIPATED SPIRIT   62

SEEDS OF LEGACY   64

NOT WITH ONE HEAD   66

SWEET SUGARCANE   67

FORGIVE	68
EAT AN ELEPHANT	70
MIND THE SNAKE PIT	71
RESPECT THE GREAT	72
EAT WITH THE KING	73
A SAGE'S COUNSEL	74
THE RAIN'S EMBRACE	75
COUNSEL	76
THE RAIN'S EMBRACE	78
LESSONS IN THE FALL	80
THE SWEETNESS WITHIN	82
DAWN'S EMBRACE	83
AWAKENING WITH THE DAWN	84
MOTHER OCEAN, AFRICA'S EMBRACE	86
CALLY'S ENCHANTING CHARM	88
THE STRENGTH OF HARD WORK	90
THE GIFT OF HOT YAM	92
BLACK SAILOR	94

Dedication

TO MOTHER, Esther Inyang

One woman who went through the challenges of impecuniousness in support of my education

RETURN TO AFRICA

Behold the beckoning call of destiny'svoice,
Emerging like a golden sunrise, rejoice!
Once again, the radiance of the sun gracesour land,
Guiding our paths, awakening dreamslong
banned.

In the tapestry of twilight, the highermoon ascends,
Casting its glow, the darkness it amends.
Africa, cherished and adored with fervent
love, your shadows transformed, a symphonyabove.

Gone is the trespasser, expelled without atrace,
Love rekindled, embraces in everyembrace.
Let us unite, as one Africa, our heartsentwined,
Love's nectar flows, a potion divine.

Seeking love's embrace? Come hither,homeward
bound, In Africa's embrace, true love shall befound.
For love resides within this sacred soil, A treasure to
share, for all hearts to embroil.

6

Life's sweetness blooms within thesehallowed
grounds,

No chains to bind, liberation resounds. Laughter
dances upon lips once muted, A home rediscovered,
jubilantly reputed

No longer ensnared in the grip of greed'svice,
Freedom's symphony sings, a paradise twice.
Our wives, the pillars of pride and grace,our
children roam, reveling in their ownembrace.

Together we pray, our voices intertwine,
empowering each other, transcending time.
Africa, we have returned, here to stay,In unity, love,
and prosperity's array.

LEGACY OF SURVIVAL

In downtowns riverside, a poignant feeling stirs,
Where the ocean's voice echoes with somber slurs.
The blood of black souls paints a tragic tale, Yet we
endure, entwined in their haunting trail.

Through tears shed by the oppressed, the Negroes
weep, Yet they cleanse their wounds in rivers vast
and deep. In the tender embrace of young dawn's
gentle glow, They seek solace, a place where they
may bestow.

But alas, doors remained shut, hearts blind andcold,
Their ebony skin a barrier, stories untold. Within the
angles of a pyramid's resolute frame,A Nile's ancient
whispers fueled their fiery flame.

They heard their brethren's songs on mountaintops
high, Beside the flowing river, where black spirits lie.
Unified, they surged forth,joining the chariots'
dance, Struggling as one, a symphony of resilience.

In foreign lands, far from their ancestral abode,
Surrounded by walls of whiteness, they toiled and
strove. Whispers from the spirits echoed through
their veins,
"Let survivors reign, even as enslaved remains."

Today, the Negroes stand tall, their legacy alive, A
testament to their strength, as they continue to
thrive. For they are more than the chains that once
held them tight, Their spirits soar, defying darkness
with resplendent light.

REKINDLED BY NATURE

In your presence, I rediscover my essence, where nature's touch revives my very essence.You bestow upon me pure sustenance divine, A feast adorned with flavors nature designed.

From the skilled hands of a true mother's grace, savor each morsel, nature's embrace.
After years spent under a surgeon's decree,I now taste the essence of true harmony.

Deep within me, a symphony awakens anew, nourished by the natural, I feel vibrant and true.
You have bestowed upon me the finest of fare, transforming me into a natural man beyond compare.

No longer confined to the realm of the ordinary,In your embrace, I transcend the customary. For nature's touch has rekindled my inner flame, Empowering me with a newfound sense of acclaim.

HARMONIES OF THE BAOBAB

...A Ghanaian fusion

Akans dwell in the heart of Ghana, where Their
wisdom, like kente, weaves tales to tell. From
coastal Ga to Dagomba's northern light,we see
tribes dance, their spirits taking flight.

Underneath the shade of mighty Baobab trees,Ewe
women weave stories in vibrant melodies.

Dagombas, with drums, summon the ancientfire,
And Ga-Adangbes celebrate, their joy never tires.

In markets bustling with life's vibrant hues, Fante
tongues mingle with the morning dew.Preserving the
believes, like pots crafted withcare,
Ghana's soul thrives in every rhythmic flare.

From the first yam's harvest to the Fire's fierce
glow,Ghana's essence, like the savannah's flow,
Is a symphony of voices, a tapestry of grace,an ode
to the land where cultures embrace?

11

From the celebration of their forefathers of old,To
the fervent chants where faith is told, Ghana's spirit
dances in the church's glow, And in the

mosques where prayers softly flow.

Yet, amidst the songs, superstitions roam, In
whispers of such believes, they find their home.
But Ghana's heart beats with a steady hand,As
customs weave a curtain across the land.

In every festival, in every feast,
From the north to the south, from west to east,
Ghana's rainbow shines with colors bright, A
testament to its people's endless light.

SWEETNESS PERSONIFIED

Nene, you embody a sweetness divine, Sweeter than sugarcane, a taste so fine.
Oh, queen of Africa, on nature's playground,Hand in hand, we dance, our love unbound.

Africana, the epitome of sweet delight, You fill my days with joy, morning to night. As we sway in harmony, our souls entwined, Your lips, a symphony, leaving me enthralled, refined.

Endowed with grace, your kisses a treasure ofvalues, Even long after, their honey I still savor. Your sweetest love, a gift beyond compare,My beloved, Africana, I forever cherish anddeclare.

Thank you, my sweetheart, for being true, In every chapter of my life, it's you I pursue.With each passing moment, our love anew,
Africana, our destinies forever intertwined, it's true.

THE RISE OF AFURIKA

Oh, land of boundless prosperity, Beacon of hope for
ages yet to be,
A F R U R I K A, resounding and bold, though
stripped, your spirit cannot be sold.

They sought to bring you shame, a tarnishedname,
Yet you refused to bear the burden of blame. Pushed
down, but you sprang up with steadfastmight,
Resilient and relentless, a beacon of light.

For a better tomorrow, you press on, In your
radiance, the beauty of a new dawn.Your culture, a
tapestry of enchanting grace,
Unmatched in its splendor, an ancient embrace.
Blessed is your land, abundant and fertile, where
bountiful harvests paint a vivid mural. Your
creativity, a wellspring that knows no end,an
unmatched tapestry, a gift to transcend.

A F U R I K A, embrace your divine calling, For you
are destined for greatness, continuallysoaring.

14

Lift your head high, let your spirit ascend,Divinity awaits, for you to transcend.

For God has blessed you with immeasurable might,
Arise, shine, and bathe in the celestial light.
The world awaits your triumph, your destiny's call,A F U R I K A, rise and stand tall.

THE BEAUTY OF MY BLACK SKIN

No charcoal rubbed upon my flesh, To adorn this
beauty, bold and fresh.
I am simply original, unadorned,
A testament to nature's grace, adorned.

Crafted by the hands of the great creator,My black
skin, a divine nature.
Foreign soldiers tempted, enticed, To change my
hue, my beauty prized.

They sought to mold me, a counterfeit of real,A
facade of beauty, a false appeal.
Abasiakan, I reject their lure, My black skin, pure
and secure.

Do not seduce me with your potions, dear,To change
my skin, for I hold it dear.
Tufiakwa, like Alice's blinder's doom, Beware the
path that leads to a fading bloom.
Do not anoint me with concoctions vile,African kin,

16

let's cherish our own style. For this black skin is a
fertile ground, Bearing the fruit of greatness
profound.

In its ebony embrace, fertility thrives, Productive,
abundant, where life survives.
I celebrate each black skin, divine, A rare gift
bestowed upon mankind.

Nature's offering, a symbol of pride, Black is
beautiful, let the world decide. In this celebration,
the West shall see, The power, the beauty, that
black can be.

17

THE MIDNIGHT LAMENT

As midnight drew near,
I whispered to Nene, my dear,Together, let us offer
a prayer,In the depths of our despair.

Kneeling with hands raised high, We closed the
doors, stifling the cry.
Nene wept with fervent passion, Oh, ABASIETTE,
hear our supplication.

A promise once made, never to forsake, If we place
our trust, in you we partake.I joined in the cry,
united in our plea, Believing our passion will set us
free.
Together we wept, our voices entwined, Seeking
change of fortunes, a fate redefined.
From worst to good, to be the very best,A chance to
live, a life divinely blessed.

With unwavering faith in the Almighty above, We
cry out for His grace, not our strength thereof.
In Africa, our hearts find solace and belief, That
through prayer and tears, we'll find relief.

SERENADE OF KENYA

In the cradle of Africa, where stories are spun,Lies
Kenya, a symphony beneath the sun.
A tapestry of cultures, woven with care, Each
thread a testament, beyond compare.

From the rhythmic beats of Nairobi's streets,To the
ancient whispers where history meets.
A dance of tradition, a melody of song,Where echoes
of the past still belong.

In the shadow of Kilimanjaro, proud and tall,Where
Maasai warriors heed nature's call.
Their chants echo across the vast expanse,A dance of
pride, a warrior's dance.

From the shores of Lamu to Turkana's sands,Where
petroglyphs etch tales of distant lands.
Each stroke a story, each line a rhyme,A tribute to
a forgotten time.

19

In the words of Ngugi, the poet's pen, Kenya's story
unfolds, again and again.
Through literature's lens, we see the truth,Of a
nation's journey, from age to youth.

In music's embrace, Kenya finds its voice, From
benga to hip-hop, each beat a choice.
The guitar's lament, the drum's refrain,Echoes of
resilience, in joy and pain.

And in the art that adorns Kenya's walls,From cave
paintings to modern halls.
A reflection of a people, proud and strong,In colors
vibrant, in stories long.

So let us raise our voices, in praise and song,To
Kenya, where the spirit belongs.
In the serenade of cultures, let us find, The
heartbeat of a nation, in unity entwined.

THE UNHEARD MAN

Within me, emotions stir and dwell,A man you treat
as if under a spell.
While you sleep soundly through the night,I toil and
burn, my soul in constant fight.

At sunrise, I yearn to be released,
To embrace my wife and children, find inner peace.
With eyes bloodshot from weariness and strain, Yet
in my sorrow, I remain humane, not in vain.

Nothing is new under the sun, I perceive, You sow
wickedness, and likewise, you receive.
So, choose your path wisely, with thoughtful heed,
Between goodness and darkness, take your lead.

21

THE GUARDIANS EMBRACE

In the vessel of transformation, A symbol of
transcendent might,The Guardian's Embrace,
Ignites the flame of Africa's light.

Orphaned, yet undaunted, The jar's fragility
concealed, In its whispers, secrets unfold,The
guardian's shield revealed.

Bound by the chain of time, This sacred oil holds the
key, To lubricate the wheels of fate,And shape
Africa's legacy.
For if this vessel should break,A void would haunt
the land,
The harmony of existence disrupted, Destinies
undone by fate's cruel hand.

Preserve this precious elixir, For in its depths lies
hidden sway, Let no careless act shatter its grace,Or
Africa's spirit will begin to fray.

SYMPHONY OF ECHOING DRUMS

Drums, the heartbeat of the land,Resounding with
ancestral might,Symbolic echoes of unity,
Ignite Africa's sacred flight.

Harmonious melodies of ancient days,through
rhythms, stories are told,A symphony of souls
entwined, Where the heart's desires unfold.

In the dance of ebony and gold, Traditions
interwoven, never undone,Africa's kaleidoscope
unfurls, Underneath the resplendent sun.

The pulse of drums, relentless and true,transcending
borders, breaking chains, they unify the scattered
tribes, kindling strength that forever remains.

Oh, let the drums forever echo,
In the hearts of Africa's sons and daughters,For in
their rhythmic cadence lies,
The soul of a continent's eternal waters.

23

WHISPERS OF THE BAOBAB TREE

Beneath the ancient Baobab's shade,Wisdom's secrets
softly breathe,A living monument of bygone days,
Where Africa's spirit finds reprieve.

Its branches, arms outstretched,Hold tales of old,
untold by time,Each leaf a sacred parchment,
Enchanting whispers, a mystical chime.

Gnarled and weathered, the tree stands tall,A
guardian of ancestral grace,
Its roots dig deep, anchoring souls,Nurturing Africa's
sacred embrace.

In the whispers of the Baobab's breeze,Lies the
essence of Africa's core, Listen closely, oh seeker of
truth, Unlock the wisdom, forevermore.

For within this ancient arboreal tome, Lies the
tapestry of Africa's past, Guiding the present,
shaping the future, A testament that will forever
last.

24

BECAUSE OF AFRICA

Savannas stretch wide across Mama's land, Multi-
colored of nations, with history's pride.
From the Nile's ancient flow to the Sahara's golden
sand,Each comer, each rhythm, enriches our lands.

Because of Africa, the world has seen light, From
the mighty Niger to the Congo's fierce might.
Egypt's pyramids stand tall, a beacon of old,Guiding
civilizations, yet stories untold.

Ghana's gold, Mali's wealth, untold treasures,Our
kingdoms echoes, tales of old, Caravans crossing,
trading with glee, Bringing riches afar, across land
and sea.

Zimbabwe's Great Zimbabwe, a marvel to behold,
Built with skill and wisdom.
Ethiopia's Axum, Lalibela's grace, Churches hewn
from stone, a sacred place.

25

The world has thrived, through the strides of Africa,
From Timbuktu's libraries, knowledge derived.
Carthage's legacy, Phoenician might, Sailing distant
seas, under starry night.

South Africa's diamonds, sparkling bright,Forged in
earth's depths, a dazzling sight. Morocco's artisans,
weaving dreams in silk,Spreading beauty afar,
through every ilk.

Because of Africa, America's heart beats,With

rhythms of Congo, melodies sweet.
From blues in Mississippi to jazz in New York,African
roots run deep, an unbreakable fork.

Europe's cities adorned with African art,tapestry of
cultures, each playing its parFrom London's diversity
to Paris' allure, Africa's influence, forever endure.

Asia's spices, a scent from afar, raded along ancient
routes, a guiding star.

From the Silk Road's tales to India's spice trade,
Africa's bounty, in every shade.

Nile's ancient beauty flows through Sahara's vast
expanse,
Each land, each story, a timeless dance.
Because of Africa, the world finds its beat, From
Nigeria's rhythms to South Africa's heat.Drums
echoing in Lagos, Johannesburg's song, A symphony
of cultures, where all belong.

Nigeria's resilience, a beacon of hope, In the face of
challenges, they boldly cope. From Nollywood's tales
to Afrobeat's sway,
African ingenuity, lighting the way.

South Africa's rainbow, a symbol of unity, From
Cape Town's beauty to Durban's serenity.
In the struggle for freedom, they stood tall,
Apartheid's downfall, heard by all.

From the pyramids of Egypt to the plains of Kenya,

27

Africa's heritage, a treasure to carry.

In every corner, in every land,African pride, forever
grand. Because of Africa, the world finds its soul,
In the stories untold, in the dreams that roll.
From the shores of Ghana to the peaks of
Kilimanjaro,

A continent's legacy, shining bright as a star.
Remember to remember AFRICA
Home for all

Because of Africa, our timeless treasure.
The world strives, and Unity survives.

JUST LIKE THAT

The shattered Illusions

Oh, when she shatteredMy love, pure and true,For
the slightest offense,A dove I once knew.
In an instant, it vanished, Like a dream slipping
away,Leaving me bewildered, Emotions in disarray.

She claimed it was revenge, With reasons
undisclosed, Within the walls of my home,Her
intentions undisclosed.
I couldn't comprehend Her sudden change of heart,
For I believed she stood by me,
But she tore us apart.

A concerned friend inquired, pleading for the truth
to unfold,Yet, when she spoke her words,I turned
away, my face cold.
For she left me abruptly, Blaming it on my
mother's sway,Her departure broke my soul, Leaving
me wounded that day.

I had given my all, Striving to provide and care,

29

Walking the streets of Texas,
To ensure we had enough to share.
But when her anger flared, She discarded my acts of
love,

Accusing another of understanding,More than I ever
could thereof. She walked away without hesitation,
Leaving me bewildered, just like that,And so, I
resolved within myself,

I won't be hurt by such an act.
She claimed she loved her mother,More than the
love I bestowed, For her advice directed her,
To learn a trade, as tradition showed.

In Africa, women uplift, Extending a helping hand,
A virtuous woman supporting a man,Building a
foundation on love's sand.

But she questioned her worth, As a first-class
graduate of acclaim,She departed on her own path,
Leaving me in sorrow and shame.

30

Now she's gone, lost to me, Where she went, I
cannot say,I pray for our unborn child,
A safe arrival, come what may.

For I have made a decision, To start my life afresh,
anew, I will not let her betrayal define me,I'll rebuild
and bid the pain adieu.

This morning, after prayer,I embraced a brand-
new start,Letting go of the past's chains,
Rekindling hope within my heart.
I cannot sacrifice myself, For one who never truly
cared,

I embark on a journey of self-love,Leaving behind a
love impaired.

And so, I rise from the ashes, Leaving shattered
illusions behind,Embracing a future of strength, With
newfound purpose, I find.

Just like that, I forge ahead, Leaving behind the
pain's cruel art,Resilient and determined,
To reclaim my wounded heart.

31

IN THE REALM OF DREAMS

In a world beyond, she dreams, To tame
grasshoppers, or so it seems.
"ATAKTAK," So she softly calls, No more shall
natives be foreign thralls.

On our soil, Mama has declared, No more alien
status to be shared.
She longs to lay her bed in freedom's embrace,
Witness her children grow, each a hero in theirspace.

In their homeland, they shall thrive,Not as
strangers, but masters alive.This place, a divine gift
bestowed,
Next time, when I return, my blackness will beboldly
showed.

I shall shake the tables, challenge the norms, Unfurl
my wings, like an eagle, I'll transform.
In the realm of dreams, where possibilities reside,I'll
soar to heights unrestrained, with unwaveringpride.

32

THE SMILE REBORN

In the realm of love's enigma, a song unfolds,Heard
in the nocturnal hours, secrets untold. A symphony
weaves through the veil of night,
Unveiling magic, igniting smiles with sheer delight.

Oh, how this enchanting melody casts its spell,
Breathing life into my smile, a tale to tell.
As I slumber, it serenades my deepest sleep,
Unveiling rhythms that my heart longs to keep.

Words fail to capture the essence it imparts, For it
transcends mortal language, touching ourhearts.
I smile to the rhythm of a sweet, elusive tune,Lost in
the lyrics, memories of us strewn.
In dreams, we dance, entwined in mystic embrace,
As the magic music swirls, time finds no trace.
In this ethereal realm, I dare to be your king, Your

heart, my throne, where eternal love shall sing.
No distance can quell the bond we share, For my
heart beholds you, no matter where. This love

33

transcends mere mystery and rhyme, For soon, I
shall come, to claim you, for all time.

To love and be loved, an everlasting vow, As we
unite, our souls' yearnings shall enow. In the
tapestry of destiny, we'll find our way,Together we'll
dwell, forever, come what may.

THE AFRICAN HARVEST

Serve me Abacha, the African delight, With mixed
leaves, a fusion that ignites. A symphony of natural
flavors, divine, Reviving the senses, life's essence to
define.

Blend those leaves, potent in their cure,
Transforming, energizing, pure and sure.
Satisfy my hunger, awaken my zeal, For this African
salad, my spirit shall heal.

Let me savor each bite, nourishing and true,Superior
to any tonic, the claims I eschew. Quench my thirst,
not with sugary drinks indisguise,

But with the juice of nature's bounty, my prize.
Give me the African kind of salad, I beseech, A
medley of vegetables, their virtues within reach.
This is a homecoming, dear friends, you see, We've
left behind the best, but now we shall feast.

35

Return to the embrace of our roots, my kin, Indulge
in the flavors that resonate deep within.
Eat of the best, replenish body and soul,Then
venture forth, enriched and whole.

36

EPIC OF BEAUTY

In the depths of Africa's embrace, Where wisdom
and wealth interlace,I delve into my roots, so dear,
A treasure trove of beauty clear.

For wisdom, the fairest friend of all,Whose radiance
can never fall,
I tread the path that leads me true,To future riches,
old and new.

In decency, respect, and love,I draw from ancestors
above,
Their footsteps guide me on my way,To surpass
them and seize the day.

Coveting wisdom, a priceless wealth,I cherish its
essence, in utmost stealth,For in its pursuit, I aim to
lead,
To be a beacon, others heed.
Amidst the chatter, I choose to hear, The whispers
of wisdom, crystal clear,For in the heart of the
sagacious wise,Lies silent

37

riches, no disguise.

Like tranquil waters, calm and pure,A fortune
immense, forever secure, For the generations yet
to come, A legacy of wisdom, never undone.

Let these verses ignite your imagination,Imbued with
symbolism and evocation, Africa's symbols, vivid and
grand,
In poetic embrace, we firmly stand.

DON'T BREAK THE JAR OF OIL

Treasure the jar, a vessel rare, Guard the oil, handle with utmost care.For oil holds power, importance untold,

No mere plaything, but a substance of gold. Within its drops, possibilities reside, Lubricating the wheels where destiny rides.

Like a symbol of excellence, it is held,preserve its essence, let it unfold. An orphan's touch, gentle and kind, Protects the jar, ensuring it won't find Destruction's path, shattered and spilled,For in its preservation, destiny is fulfilled.

Africa's wheels would cease to turn, If our pots of oil were to break and burn. Humanity's service, wealth, and gain,Rests upon the oil's abundant reign.

With great significance, your jar does hold,Affecting the world, as its story unfolds. So cherish the oil, safeguard its worth, For a shattered pot disrupts life's mirth.

39

ELYSIAN AND ABASSINIA
..Ethiopia's Symphony of Time

Through the cradle of ancient whispers, time
unfurls,

There stands, a symphony of otherworldly swirls,
A realm where shadows dance, and dreams embark,
In the heart of Abyssinia, where spirits embark.

From the sacred heights of Axum's silent stones,To
Lalibela's carved sanctuaries, where history intones,
Echoes of eternity linger, in every hallowed hall,A
chorus of ages, where destiny's call.

Amidst the rifts where past and present align,
Ethiopia's spirit, a beacon divine,
A tapestry woven with threads of grace, In the
symphony of life, in this sacred space.

40

From the Nile's gentle flow to the mountains high,
Ethiopia's story, painted across the sky,
In hues of courage, in shades of gold,A testament to
the tales that unfold.

In Ethiopia's embrace, where legends rise,A journey
of souls, under starlit skies,
In every breath, in every rhyme, Elysian echoes,
through the sands of time.

41

GO FOR MORE

Seek not just knowledge, but wisdom profound,For
in the wise, true solutions are found.
The knowledgeable may falter, so we say, For
wisdom alone withstands crisis's sway.

Knowledge without wisdom is like water's fate,Lost
in the desert, unable to sate.
When troubles arise, and challenges loom,The wise
among us shall truly bloom.

Amidst the knowledgeable and those with might,
Fearful of reasoning, their minds take flight.
But wisdom, unlike money's transient hold,In times
of crisis, shines brightest and bold.

For only the wise can build bridges strong,Spanning
divides where we may belong. While the foolish erect
dams in their pride,The wise alone help us safely
stride.

So go forth, seek knowledge, yes, but strive,For
wisdom's essence to truly arrive.

42

In crisis and calm, let wisdom prevail,A guiding
light, when all else may fail.

43

EASY NANA

Why rush to jump across the river wide, When
through crawling, a child learns to stride?
Easy, dear Nana, let learning expand,
For great souls wield knowledge with a gentle hand.

Wealth may fade, like an ephemeral tide, But
learning, when nurtured, continues to guide.
Open your eyes to the truth held within, For
accidental learning brings only chagrin.

In accidents, wounds may come to bear, Yet those
who learn well, knowledge will share.Just as a
monkey leaps from tree to tree,Through effort,
Nana, you too can be free.

Haba, dear Nana, can't you perceive?
Skills are honed when trees we do cleave.
Wise lessons were crafted by sagacious minds,To

teach fools the folly of being unrefined.

So embrace the wisdom these lessons bestow, And
let foolishness within you no longer grow.
For learning is the key to break free, To become
wiser, enlightened, as can be.

45

THE TANZANIAN WOMAN

Behold the Tanzanian woman, adorned with grace,
Wisdom adorning her like a Native American's
embrace.
She roams the town with pride on display,
Announcing her beliefs through what she conveys.

Like the Native American, she adores the show,
Revealing her knowledge in the things she bestow.
This Tanzanian friend, wrapped in vibrant hues,
Bold-patterned wraps, skirts that she chooses.

Just as Nene in Nigeria, skillfully creates, Jewelry
sold at Okombegallery's lively gates.So does this
Tanzanian, market her beliefs,
A tapestry of expression, like shimmering reef.

Like Opiyo in Kenya, who proudly displays, Her
goods at the bustling Savannah market's maze.She
holds her hometown dear, with heartfelt pride,

Machakos, a small Kenyan town where she does

reside.

This Tanzanian, akin to an orange and yellow's glow,
Brightens the streets, a Swahili beauty in tow.
She doesn't celebrate war, but weeps for peace, For
she loves nature's allure, where serenity findsrelease.

In her presence, one feels tranquility's call,A
testament to her spirit, standing tall. The Tanzanian
woman, a symbol of grace,
Radiating wisdom, with every step and embrace.

47

NKECHI

Nkechi, a soul of African grace, Amidst the maids,
she found her place.
Choosing a path that set her apart, Her presence
pleased the king's noble heart.

Like the sun's rays, her radiance glowed, With
African symbols, her spirit bestowed.
Adorned in kente, vibrant and bold, She worked
diligently, a story untold.

In her stride, the rhythm of the drums, Her spirit
soared, Africa's anthem hums.
Each step, a dance, full of elegance and flair, She
embodied the essence of culture rare.

Her hands, skilled like a weaver's loom, Crafted
beauty, turning threads into bloom.
Just as Adinkra symbols grace the cloth,
Her workmanship displayed with passion and troth.
Nkechi, the embodiment of strength and grace, A
symbol of African spirit, in every embrace. She

carved her own path, against the tide, Bridging

worlds, with heritage as her guide.

In the eyes of the king, she found her worth,A jewel
of Africa, a treasure unearthed.
Nkechi, a name that echoes through time,Her legacy
shines, like the sun's prime.

For she lived unique, amid the maids' clan, Her
presence resonating, like an ancient plan.Nkechi, an
emblem of resilience and pride,
A symbol of Africa's spirit, reaching far and wide.

49

ONE STEP AFTER THE OTHER

Do not leap blindly into the unknown's abyss,
Beware of wounds inflicted, the pain that persists.
Hold back your urge, don't rush headlong,Ponder
the situation, for it may be wrong.

Do not be a fool, testing depths in haste, With both
feet diving, recklessness embraced.
Instead, take measured steps, deliberate and wise,
Unveil the depth gradually, like the sunrise.

One step after another, proceed with care,Each
cautious move, a journey to prepare. Try the depth
slowly, step by step, you see,

Unveiling truths, gaining wisdom, wild and free.
With each passing day, knowledge is won,
Navigating the path to destiny, under the sun.For
the voyage unfolds, like a tapestry grand, Revealing
life's purpose, in Africa's sacred land.

Through imagery and symbols, we find our way,

50

African spirit guides us, night and day.
So let patience guide you, as you take each stride,
One step after the other, with destiny as your guide.

51

LEARN TO BE BETTER

Embrace the quest for knowledge's gain, In Africa,
even little things shall train. For what you acquire
becomes your own,A treasure everlasting, firmly
sown.

Own it incessantly, let it reside, Within your being, a
constant guide. But knowledge alone is not enough,
Put it to use, let actions be your stuff.

From these actions, abundant gain, A life worth
praising, free from disdain.A great existence,
adorned with esteem,
Nurtured by knowledge, like a garden's theme.
For knowledge uncultivated, like barren land,Yields
no harvest, no fruits to command.
Learn to cultivate, tend with care,The seeds of
wisdom, everywhere.

Live life better, with the gifts it brings, A bountiful
harvest, where fulfillment sings. Reap the rewards of
your knowledge's might,As you journey through
Africa's vibrant light.

52

THE RESEMBLANCE

In nature's design, a truth prevails, A crab birthing a bird, the story derails.For each belongs to a distinct domain, Okoto and Anoma, their paths remain.

A child must bear the resemblance true, In looks and character, through and through.For if you do not reflect your creator's grace,Whom shall you resemble, in life's embrace?

Like the sun, radiating light so bright, Or the moon, glowing in tranquil night, We carry the echoes of our origins' trace, A reflection of our roots, a divine embrace.
In Africa's tapestry, this truth holds strong, Resembling the ancestors who came along. Their legacy woven within our very core,

Guiding us, inspiring us, forevermore.

So let the resemblance shine forth with pride, Honoring the past, while forging our stride.

53

For in embracing our creator's design, We find
purpose and meaning, truly divine.

54

CLIMB A GOOD TREE

In unity, we rally for a noble quest, Against
destruction and corruption's behest. If you dare to
ascend a tree of purpose strong,
We'll stand by your side, urging you along.

Climb that tree with determination's flame, Where
beautiful fruits and goodness reclaim. For the
harvest awaits, abundant and grand,Not just for
yourself, but for society's hand.

The society and its elders shall lend their support,
Guiding your ascent, their wisdom will exhort.
Together we'll push, to ensure you reach the top,
Aiming for the apex, where dreams never stop. The
society and its elders shall lend their support,
Guiding your ascent, their wisdom will exhort.
Together we'll push, to ensure you reach the top,
Aiming for the apex, where dreams never stop.

In the heart of Africa, a beacon does shine,The mark
of a youth, with virtues so fine. Identified by their
noble deeds and grace,A testament to the African
spirit we embrace.

55

AFRICAN PARTY

In the streets, people gather with delight, Dancing
to the rhythm of the drums, day andnight.
The spirit of the drums, their vibrant beat, Guides
us towards a moment, truly complete.

Every corner of the street alive with energy,Every
corner of the street alive with energy,Hearts and
souls aflame, feeling the synergy.
The music echoes loud, reaching higher and higher,
As voices unite, singing with burning desire.
All night long, the melodies fill the air, In every
street, a celebration to share. Join our party,
embrace the joyful cheer, Eat, drink, and laugh,
casting away all fear.

Jambo, jambo, the joyful chants resound, As we sing
and jump, our voices unbound. We make our
presence heard, near and far,

Throughout the day and night, a vibrant memoir.
This timely festival, a cherished tradition, Where

56

we dance and feast with pure elation. We delight the eyes of visitors with our bliss, Inviting them to join, experience the African kiss.

Come and join us, as the new moon shines, Let your voices echo, blending with our rhymes.
All over the world, let our joy be heard, In this African party, where spirits are stirred.

57

AFRICAN RHYTHMS

Beneath the sun's embrace, they sway,A dance of
spirits, in golden ray, Morning awakens, drums
resound, Their beats, a language, profound.

Through dusty streets, they move with grace,In
syncopation, a sacred chase,
Seeking the pinnacle of harmony's flight,Guided by
drums, the pulse of the night.

Their hearts reverberate, a rhythmic thrum,Soulful
vibrations, Africa's anthem, Melodies rise, soaring
higher,
Igniting flames of ancestral fire.

In the tapestry of sound, they find release,Melting
boundaries, their spirits unleashed,Throughout the
night, their voices ring, A joyous symphony, the
songs they sing.

Come, partake in this festive embrace,Indulge in
laughter, nourish your taste,Jambo, jambo, let the

rhythm guide, We celebrate life, with every stride.

Witness the spectacle, both near and far, A vibrant
celebration, beneath moon and star,
Join us in this timeless festivity, Let our voices
echo, across land and sea.

59

THE VILLAGE'S EMBRACE

Beyond blood ties, this soul does dwell,In a village's embrace, a tale to tell, Not bound by mere biology's claim, But nurtured by a collective flame.

Across the plains of Africa's land,
A child's upbringing, a communal brand,For in this realm, we deeply believe, Society shapes the values they receive.

No single parent, in isolation, stands, It's the village's duty, their helping hands, To mold a character, both strong and kind,Every member, responsible, intertwined.

In this vibrant tapestry of togetherness,Guiding a child, a shared coalescence, From correction's firm but loving voice,To tender care, each member's choice.

A feast of wisdom, passed through the years,Gifted

60

to the child, through collective tears, Every soul invested, no matter their name, In shaping a future, lighting life's flame.

In Africa's heart, it's understood, Nourishing a child, a neighborhood, With open arms and hearts aligned, We tend to the young, as one defined.

61

EMANCIPATED SPIRIT

No longer shall the whip descend, Its echoes fading,
my spirit unbend,My blood, no elixir for your thirst,
In freedom's realm, I triumph first.

Imperfect I may be, but hear me roar, For Africa's
cause, my heart will soar, To serve, to build, my
purpose profound,No longer bound, liberation's
sound.

I've overturned the tables, reversed the game,The
oppressors' fire consumed in flame,No longer a
slave, a cog in their machine,
A new narrative emerges, vibrant and serene.

The ship ablaze, their tool of enslavement, No more
captive, I break free from containment,
I belong to Africa's sovereign embrace, A destiny
forged, a spirit unchained in grace.

Let this shared consciousness prevail,Residing within

us, a united tale,
To dwell, to thrive, within Africa's domain,A new
dawn arises, bearing Africa's reign.

In fruitful abundance, steadily we rise,Africa's
essence, a beacon that defies,For in our unity, we
hold the key,
To a future where Africa's greatness shall decree.

63

SEEDS OF LEGACY

Son of a son of a farmer

Born of the tiller's lineage, a fertile line,Son of the
soil, in heritage we find,
A farmer's blood, coursing through your veins,Bearer
of life, tending nature's domains.

Rooted in the land, where dreams take hold,Sowing
seeds of time, stories yet untold, With every furrow
turned, and every crop, A livelihood blooms, a
harvest nonstop.

Son of the soil, a visionary of dreams, Expanding
horizons, where ambition gleams,Day by day, your
vision expands wide,
To cultivate a legacy, with each stride.

Agricultural dynasties, within your sight,
Generations intertwined, their futures bright,Oh,
son of the soil, a testament you stand, A beacon of
hope, reaching out your hand.

64

Son of the soil, in your father's footsteps, And his father's father, an unbroken depth, You bring home happiness, abundance untold, A legacy of success, a dynasty to behold.

Dining and conversing with the town's elite, Yet grounded in the earth, where triumphs meet, Son of your fathers, the epitome of toil, A savior of lives, nurturer of the soil Son of a son of a farmer.

NOT WITH ONE HEAD

In the realm of belief,We shatter the notionThat a
solitary soul With a single crown
Should preside over a gatheringHow can Okombe, in
solitude, Conduct a meeting with self?

Oh, tyrant of malice, Longing to reign in perpetuity,
While the righteous one, In soliloquy, contemplates,
Shuts the door on collaboration.

Yet, let us acknowledge The semblance of a
meeting,Where, pray tell,
Did the assembly

Of sage and noble minds reside,To guide us toward
A fruitful resolution?

As my Oyinbo friend oft declares, Two heads,
entwined, bear wisdom.Hence, we beckon, "Wake,
Okombe!"For decision-making,
We crave the diverse arms,

No single being can comprise a council,Nor
determine our destiny.

66

SWEET SUGARCANE

In the realm of sweetness,Where goodness thrives,
Existence perseveres, Elusive in its pursuit.

For sweetness and virtue, Though adorned with
allure,Require arduous quests, Amidst trials and
pains,

A multitude they may be. Yet, the culmination of
good Rewards the toil endured. As sugarcane, in its
splendor,Unveils its sweetest nectar, At the junction
of sucrose, Where aspirations converge.
Having arrived,

At the longed-for abode, After ceaseless endeavors,
The enduring reward unfolds,A sweetness
everlasting.

67

FORGIVE

Ette, in his wisdom, imparted,When transgressions occur,

Seek forgiveness, if the offender you be.
And if offense befalls your soul,Bestow the gift of forgiveness. Why allow yourself to scorch In the fires of animosity,

Trading away divine inheritance,A gift bestowed by the Almighty?

Simplicity echoes through this decree:Apologize to the wounded,

When their toes are inadvertently trodden,And graciously accept their contrition, When they extend it in kind.

Let love be the creed of the ebony heart, Embracing our identity through time's embrace.
"Ette" refers to a wise figure or elder offering advice.

68

The poem emphasizes the importance of seeking and granting forgiveness.

It questions the point of harboring unforgiveness and encourages embracing the gift of forgiveness, which is seen as a divine inheritance

.

The poem promotes the notion of expressingremorse when one has wronged others and accepting apologies with grace.

It calls for love to be the cornerstone of the Black community, embracing and cherishing our collective identity throughout history.

69

EAT AN ELEPHANT

Indeed, it can be done, Though daunting it may
appear,To those lacking skill and might.

Many may dare, Yet lack the know-how.

But the audacious and creative, Can conquer the
king of the wild,Transforming the elephant's flesh,To
fill the pot of soup.

Yes, you can, Follow the cunning path,Slice it into
fragments,

For it is through incremental efforts,That the
colossal is subdued.

No matter the enormity, Of the problem at hand,
Break it down into morsels,Devour it piece by piece.

With each bit, and every step taken,The best course
unfolds,

To unravel a mighty conundrum.
Approach it gradually, Bit by bit, and step by step.

70

MIND THE SNAKE PIT

Beware the restless foot, dear soul, Why self-
destruct, why take that toll?

Refrain from busying thyself
In realms unknown, beyond thy grasp.

Why tread into the snake pit's lair, And succumb to
venom's deadly snare?

A single bite, a poisoned brew, Unleashing
consequences unforeseen.

If thy foot knows not tranquility's reign, Dangerous
paths thou shalt entertain. Regret shall cloak thy
wounded heart, Once folly's deeds have played their
part.

Then, with clarity's unveiled light,Thy foolishness
shall come to sight.

71

RESPECT THE GREAT

To attain greatness's domain, Pay homage to those
who have reigned.For in your journey's destined
course, The great ones stand as guiding force.

To forge a path toward eminence, Respect becomes
your key, your essence. Sow seeds of reverence, pure
and true, And wisdom from the great you'll accrue.

Harvest the fruits of respect sown, And
admiration in abundance shall be known.

Yet, heed this truth, now crystal clear,Disrespect
begets no honor, my dear.

72

EAT WITH THE KING

In stature small, a child so pure,Cleanses hands with water's lure,The king's table opens wide, Inviting the innocent to reside.

A spotless child, with virtues bright,Shall feast upon regal delight.

Embrace the chance, let training bloom,A gateway to fortunes yet to loom.

Through such opportunity bestowed, Great achievements shall be bestowed.

Favored, you shall be, by the king's decree, Repeatedly summoned, oh child, to see, For your noble form and virtuous ways, Delight every king, in endless praise.

73

A SAGE'S COUNSEL

A sovereign, wise and just, Adorned with counsel's
trust, His reign, a haven of peace, Guided by
wisdom's masterpiece.

For one's essence, true and rare, Is shaped by
friendships we share,The path we tread, it does
decree,The culmination of destiny.

Choose noble ways, let virtue lead, Associate with
men of noble creed, For in a circle of greatness
sown, Success and fortune shall be known.

Beware! Let not your realm be marred, By
comrades who bring naught but shards,Ill omens
whispering in the gloom,

Their counsel, a harbinger of doom.

Thus, guard your life, precious and true,From souls
aimless and misconstrued, Let purpose shape your
noble kin,
And safeguard the legacy within.

74

THE RAIN'S EMBRACE

In solitude, raindrops fall,A tale of trials, heard by
all, For challenges arrive, unasked,
Like trains on roofs, shadows cast.

Trouble, a stranger at your door,Fear not its
presence anymore,
With strength, embrace the pouring rain,Conquer
the odds that cause you pain.

Take heed from those who came before,Illuminate
the path once more,
Let troubles be outshined and fade,In the brilliance
of choices made.

75

COUNSEL

Amidst a kingdom's hallowed halls, A sovereign, wise
and just enthralls,

His throne adorned with counsel's trust, His reign, a
haven where peace is a must.

For one's true essence, rare and pure,Is shaped by
friendships we procure, The life we live, a tapestry
divine, Woven with threads of souls entwined.

Choose noble ways, let virtue guide, Associate with
hearts that won't divide, In the company of men of
noble creed, Success and fortune shall surely
proceed.

Beware! Let not your realm be marred, By
comrades who bring naught but shards,Ill omens
whispering in the gloom,

Their counsel, a harbinger of doom.
Guard your life, precious and true, From souls

76

aimless and misconstrued, With purpose as your
compass and guide,Safeguard the legacy within,
abide.

In unity lies strength, in bonds we find,The wisdom
to shape our noble mind, So let the king seek counsel
wide,
With sage advisors standing side by side.

Together, forge a realm renowned, Where harmony
and justice resound,
For a king who surrounds himself with light,Shall
lead his kingdom to glorious height.

77

THE RAIN'S EMBRACE

Don't say it is you alone who stands, Facing troubles
with trembling hands,For rain does fall in solitude,
Yet challenges come to all, not just a few.

Like trains that grace each rooftop's ledge,Trouble
knocks at every door's edge,
A stranger, unexpected and unknown, But fear not,
for strength can be shown.

Cry not when troubles come to call,Instead, rise
above and conquer all, Take hold of what is likely to
follow,
And let examples lead, in triumph, you'll wallow.
Look to those who've weathered the storm, Whose
hearts have grown resilient and warm,Draw
inspiration from their tales,

And let their light guide you through the gales.

In the face of adversity, stand tall, Let resilience and

courage be your all,Illuminate the path that lies
ahead,
Outshine the troubles with the choices you tread.

Embrace the rain's cascading embrace,Let it nourish
and grant you grace, For within its drops, strength
is found,
To conquer what life's challenges surround.

LESSONS IN THE FALL

Before you stumble, ere you trip, Reflect on what
led to that slip, Don't fixate on where you fell, But
the hidden cause, hidden well.

Look beyond the mistake's mere face, Seek the roots,
trace them with grace,For in understanding lies the
key,
To break the cycle and set you free.

Should you repeat the same old dance,Fate shall
weave a recurring trance, Bound to fall upon that
same ground, With no helping hand to be found.

My friend, it's not the place you fell, But
where the ground betrayed, rebelled, The

point of weakness, a treacherous snare,
Beware that spot, handle it with care.

Learn from the past, let wisdom ignite, Shed light

on the shadows of your plight, With knowledge gained, your path shall shift,To avoid the pitfalls that once caused rift.

Embrace the lessons in each downfall,Empower your spirit, stand tall, For it's in rising, wiser and adept, That resilience blooms, and freedom is kept.

81

THE SWEETNESS WITHIN

As honey is craved for its sweet embrace,Beyond the
bee, its essence we chase, So too, the sugar cane
stands tall,

Its sweetness revered by one and all.
From South Africa to Malawi's plain,We celebrate
your sweetness, without disdain,

Oh, cane of sugar, you hold the key,To a taste that
brings us harmony.
The wise, they see beyond the guise, Not judging by
cover or the stick's size,For it is the cane's natural
grace,

That fills our souls with a sugary embrace.
Those who judge by color, they miss,The joy of
sweetness that exists,

For you have taught me, oh, cane so fair, To look
beyond appearances and truly care.
A lesson learned, profound and true,Not to judge a
book by its hue, For just like you, oh, cane divine,
The sweetness within is what we find.

82

DAWN'S EMBRACE

Mama's voice echoes, strong and clear,Seek what you deserve, my dear, Awaken early, with purpose true,To seize the best that waits for you.

With the morning's energy, arise, Chase dreams beneath daybreak skies,She calls upon us, one and all,
To strive for greatness, stand tall.
Papa's words, like a guiding light,Encourage us to take flight, As the sun ascends its throne,
Tackle challenges, the difficult known.

In the early hours, with spirit unbound,Forge a path where success is found, Embrace the tasks that seem immense,And pave your way to opulence.

For in the dawn of life's grand quest,Lies the opportunity to be your best,So wake with purpose, greet the sun,
Let ambition guide, let greatness be won.

83

AWAKENING WITH THE DAWN

Mama's resolute voice rings out,
An anthem of guidance, there's no doubt,Search for
what you truly deserve, Awake with the sun, ready
to serve.

Rise early, seize the precious hours, Harness the
morning's potent powers,For in that sacred time of
light,
Lies the secret to reaching great heights.

She beckons us to rise and shine, Embrace the dawn,
our spirits align,With diligence, we chase our
dreams,Bathed in the early sunlight's gleams.

The world awakens, fresh and new, A canvas for us
to paint and pursue,Mama's call echoes, a gentle
plea, To harness the day's vitality.
Papa's voice resonates with might, Guiding us
through the morning's light,Run forth, my child,
alongside the sun,Seek the

84

elusive black goat to be won.

With the rising of the golden orb, A challenge awaits, a chance to absorb,The lessons found in arduous quests, To conquer obstacles, to be our best.

In earlier times, wisdom would say, Accomplish grand tasks, without delay, In youth's embrace, lay the cornerstone,
Of a life well-lived, where greatness is sown.
So heed their words, let them inspire, With hearts ablaze, set your goals higher,For the morning holds promises anew, An invitation to seize what is true.

Awaken early, with vigor and zeal, With purpose aflame, let your dreams reveal,
The path that leads to your desired fate, As you stride forward, undeterred by the weight.

In the gentle morning's tender embrace, Unveil the potential that lies in each space,Embrace the dawn, let it ignite,
The fire within, that burns ever bright.

85

MOTHER OCEAN, AFRICA'S EMBRACE

Oh, Mother, dear Mother of the ocean vast, When your call reaches us, we answer fast, Drawn to the melodic rhythm of your waves,We hasten to your shores, where solace paves.

Your refreshing waters, a balm for the soul, We sit by your side, where tranquility takes its toll,
In this paradise, your creation so divine,Africa's embrace, where hearts align.

Mother dear, oh, Mother of the deep, Your freshness, a treasure we forever keep,For no other can rival your tender caress, A symphony of serenity, we confess.
From the coast of Senegal to the Cape's embrace, Your waters bless us with unending grace, The vibrant hues of turquoise and blue,

A masterpiece of nature, so pure and true.

In your depths, secrets and wonders untold,A
myriad of life, mysteries unfold,
From vibrant corals to creatures grand,A testament
to Africa's abundant hand.

Oh, Mother Ocean, Africa's treasured gem,In your
embrace, we find peace and zen, Your endless
expanse, a source of awe, Connecting continents,
forever in awe.

We honor you, Mother, with hearts sincere, For the
sanctuary you provide, so clear, Your presence, a
testament to nature's might,A gift to cherish, both
day and night.

CALLY'S ENCHANTING CHARM

Down the path, where memories reside,I embarked
on a journey, a joyful stride,To a place where the
weather is chill, And nostalgia's presence lingers still.

Sweetest memories, like honey streams,Flow through
my mind, as in a dream,To the home by the water's
embrace, Where every December, I find solace.

Once again, this year, here I come, To that sweet
home, my heart is won,I rejoice in the warmth it
imparts,
As I embark on this journey of the heart.

For in a few days' time, the Carnival awaits,Africa's
grandest, where joy resonates,
A vibrant street party, a song-filled affair,With
friends and loved ones, united in flair.
Oh, sweet Cally, your spirit shines bright,In this
celebration, sheer delight,
I am here again, ready to embrace, The
festivities that illuminate your grace.

From the vibrant parades to music's sway,We dance
and sing, merriment's display, In your loving arms, I
find my place,
Oh, sweet Cally, your enchantment I embrace.

So let the rhythms carry us away,
In this magical moment, we find our way,To
celebrate life and cherished connection,In Cally's
embrace, love's sweet reflection.

89

THE STRENGTH OF HARD WORK

Hard work, the cornerstone of African might,A
testament to resilience, shining bright,
It does not kill the spirit of those who strive,For only
poverty has the power to deprive.

Complain not of the toil, the sweat and strain,For in
these efforts, we find our gain,
In the lands of Africa, where hard work prevails,We
sow the seeds of progress that never fails.

For after work is done, the work remains,To build a
future where abundance reigns,To bring to the table
the goods we cherish,
With hands that labor, our dreams shall flourish.

Through sunlit fields and bustling markets fair,We
pour our energies, without despair, Each task a
contribution, big or small,
To uplift our people, one and all.
The fruits of labor, they grace our plates,
Nourishing families, breaking the chains of fate,

90

Hard work, our companion, through thick and thin,
A noble endeavor

that helps us to win.

So let us embrace the calloused hands we bear, A
symbol of strength, a badge we wear,
For in the toil, the labor we invest, We forge a path
to a life that's blessed.

THE GIFT OF HOT YAM

A child's tender fingers, unharmed they rest, When
a piece of hot yam, by mother's behest,Is placed in
his palm, a loving embrace,
In Africa's land, where wisdom finds its space.

A sweet advice, like a steaming delight, May come
with fervor, with passion and might,
Yet, it does not scorch, it does not burn,Instead, it
shapes a lad, eager to learn.

In character and learning, it takes its place,
Nurturing a path to life's finest embrace, For in the
heat of guidance, love is shown, And the seeds of
greatness are gently sown.
Oh, Africa's wisdom, a treasure so rare,In every
word, a guiding flare,
To mold young hearts, to shape their fate,And

unlock a future that's truly great.
With love and care, the advice is given, A gift from
the heart, in wisdom-driven, To ignite the flame

that burns within, And guide the child towards success to win.

So let us embrace the lessons bestowed, The words of elders, like a fiery ode, For in their wisdom, we find the key, To unlock the best that life can be.

93

BLACK SAILOR

In ebony's embrace, a sailor bold, Embarking on a
voyage, untamed and untold, Through oceans vast,
to the world's far reaches,
We offer prayers, as your vessel breaches.

Bring forth treasures from distant shores,A
seafarer's soul, forever it soars, Leading the way
upon the boundless sea,
Conversing with waves, in whispered decree.

Fearlessly sail, oh valiant one, Progressive spirit
under the golden sun,With hands that fashion
dreams anew,To distant horizons, forever pursue.

Oh, sailor sublime, your mettle I adore, Confronting
sea's monsters, your spirit does roar,For you face the
unknown with courage untamed,Conqueror of
waves, forever acclaimed.
Unfurl the sails, seize the tide, Bring home treasures
from far and wide,
For you, oh sailor, carry the flame,

94

Embodying courage, forever the same.

A leader amidst the boundless sea, Whispering to waters, setting them free,To reach horizons yet unseen, Fearlessly sail, fulfill your dream.

Oh progressive soul, with hands that weave,Crafting wonders, as passions conceive, Extend your reach, explore untamed lands, Beyond the shores, where destiny stands.
Sailor of valor, my heart sings for thee,In the tempest's grip, you strive to be, The finest amongst the ocean's kin, Defying the beasts, your spirit within.

Yearning to conquer, to stand apart, To sail with prowess, mastering your art,Sailor, the sailor, our prayers we bestow,May fortune guide you wherever you go.

95